totally cool
Soapmaking
for Kids

totally cool

Soapmaking
for Kids

Marie Browning

Sterling Publishing Co., Inc.
New York

PROLIFIC IMPRESSIONS PRODUCTION STAFF:

Editor in Chief: Mickey Baskett
Copy Editor: Phyllis Mueller
Graphics: Dianne Miller, Karen Turpin
Styling: Kirsten Jones
Photography: Jerry Mucklow, John Yanyshyn
Administration: Jim Baskett

Every effort has been made to insure that the information presented is accurate. Since we have no control over physical conditions, individual skills, or chosen tools and products, the publisher disclaims any liability for injuries, losses, untoward results, or any other damages which may result from the use of the information in this book. Thoroughly read the instructions for all products used to complete the projects in this book, paying particular attention to all cautions and warnings shown for that product to ensure their proper and safe use.

Library of Congress Cataloging-in-Publication Data:

Browning, Marie.
   Totally cool soapmaking for kids / Marie Browning.
      p. cm.
   Includes index.
   ISBN 1-4027-0641-3
   1. Soap. I. Title.
TP991 .B788 2003
668'.12--dc22

2003015839

10 9 8 7 6 5 4 3 2 1

Published in paperback in 2005 by Sterling Publishing Co., Inc.
387 Park Avenue South, New York, N.Y. 10016
© 2004 by Prolific Impressions, Inc.

Produced by Prolific Impressions, Inc.
160 South Candler St., Decatur, GA 30030

Distributed in Canada by Sterling Publishing
C/o Canadian Manda Group, 165 Dufferin Street
Toronto, Ontario, Canada M6K 3H6
Distributed in Great Britain and Europe by Chris Lloyd at Orca Book
Services, Stanley House, Fleets Lane, Poole BH15 3AJ, England
Distributed in Australia by Capricorn Link (Australia) Pty. Ltd.
P.O. Box 704, Windsor, NSW 2756, Australia
Printed in China
All rights reserved
Sterling ISBN 1-4027-0641-3 Hardcover
          ISBN 1-4027-2242-7 Paperback

ACKNOWLEDGEMENTS

My warmest thanks to everyone who helped and supported me with this book – your thoughtfulness will always be remembered:

- Mrs. Bender's grade 6 class at Bayside Middle School for letting me test the techniques and recipes with them.
- My excellent models, Olivia, Tysann, and Julia, for being the best behaved and cutest ever! Thanks for spending a whole day of your spring break to help me.
- Photographer John Yanyshyn – it's always a pleasure to work with you!
- Gloria Davenport, my assistant.
- Mickey Baskett, my editor – Thanks again for all your support and encouragement.
- Scott, my wonderful husband, who lives with the house smelling so fragrant after a day of experimenting.
- Katelyn, Lena, and Jonathan, my wonderful children, for their patience and suggestions and for testing of all the projects in their baths!

Marie Browning would also like to thank the following companies for their generous contributions of product and support:

Aquarius Aromatherapy & Soap, Mission, BC, Canada, www.aquariusaroma-soap.com, *On-line suppliers of melt and pour soap bases, molds, fragrances, colorants, additives, inclusions, oils, and packaging and information on all aspects of soapmaking.*

Environmental Technology, Inc., Fields Landing, CA, www.eti-usa.com, *Manufacturer of Fields Landing Soap Factory melt and pour soap bases, plastic tube molds, tray molds, fragrances, and colorants.*

Image Hill, North Kansas City, MO, ww.soapexpressions.com, *Manufacturer of Soap Expressions melt and pour soap bases, soap cubes, soap cutters, molds, fragrances, colorants, additives, soap kits, and lip balm kits.*

Life of the Party, North Brunswick, NJ, www.soapplace.com, *Manufacturer of melt and pour soap bases, molds, fragrances, colorants, additives, and soap kits.*

SKS Bottle & Packaging, Inc., Mechanville, NY, www.sks-bottle.com, *On-line supplier of bulk plastic bottles, jars, aluminum tins, balm containers, and premium packaging for fragrance crafts.*

TKB Trading, Oakland, CA, www.tkbtrading.com, *On-line supplier of melt and pour soap bases, molds, fragrances, colorants, additives, inclusions, oils, and information on all aspects of soapmaking and manufacturer of high-quality soap colorants.*

Xyron, Inc., Scottsdale, AZ, www. xyron.com, *Manufacturer of adhesive application and laminating machines.*

Welcome!

to the world of fragrance fun! This book was designed to give you lots of fun projects to share with children in small or large groups. In creating it, I have drawn on my many years of teaching fragrance crafts, and I've included exciting and successful projects to do with children ages 7 to 12. I am thrilled to be able to share them with you.

The projects include instructions for making soaps (both molded bars and liquid soap), solid bath fizzies, bath salts, body powders, and balms, complete with step-by-step instructions and recipes. Packaging hints and ideas are also offered.

The soapmaking projects are made with melt and pour soap bases, which are easy to obtain and use. These soap bases have been formulated so they can be melted in a microwave oven, poured into molds, and cured – all in one day! This method of soapmaking does not include exposure to harsh chemicals such as lye, and it is safe and simple.

Soapmaking and fragrance crafting are great activities for families, classrooms, clubs, camp, and church groups. In my experience, kids find them to be fun activities. Additionally, they learn something and, when they are finished, there's the tangible reward of using or giving what they have made!

Marie Browning and Olivia, Tysann & Julia, who helped make the projects in this book

Table of Contents

Before You Get Started...
What You Should Know About Fragrance Crafting

SAFETY FIRST

- **Keep melted soap away from young children.** When working with melted soap, be careful and *always* be sure an adult is on hand to supervise. Melted soap can be very hot and if it contacts skin, blisters or burns may result. If hot soap is spilled on the skin, place the exposed area in cold water immediately.

- **Prevent soap from overheating.** Overheating can cause soap to boil, overflow the cup, and spill over onto your hand. To prevent overheating, heat the soap in small intervals and mix it to cool before letting children pour it into molds.

- **Cut soap carefully.** The soap is easy to cut. Let children cut the soap with inexpensive knives that are not very sharp. Make sure they cut on a wooden or plastic cutting board and their hands are dry to prevent slipping.

- Be careful when choosing plastic containers for molding your soaps. Some cannot take the high temperature of the melted soap and can melt and collapse, spilling the hot soap.

- **Clean up spills right away.** Spilled soap or oil can cause dangerous falls. If you accidentally spill the liquid soap or oil while working, clean it up immediately to prevent slipping. The soap will solidify quickly – you can scrape it up, and then wash the area well.

- **Always label your products.** Clearly label your finished products with the contents and instructions for use. If you don't (since some of these soaps look and smell so yummy!), someone might mistake them for food.

- **Use only safe ingredients.** Always use recommended, safe ingredients. Just because an ingredient is natural, it doesn't mean it is safe to use in your soap.

- Ocassionally, some of the steps in the project instructions will require an **adult** to closely supervise or carry out the step entirely. These steps are noted by the symbol shown here.

ABOUT YOUR SUPPLIES

Supplies you need for fragrance crafting are easy to find at crafts stores, from online suppliers, and at grocery and health food stores.

For soap-making, the most important ingredient is the soap base. Melt & Pour Soap Bases are easy and fun to use. You will also need Molds for molding the soap into squares, rectangles and fun shapes. Fragrance oils, additives, and colorants will also make your soap fun to use.

This book also includes projects such as making bubble bath, lip balm, bath salts and other personal care products. Many of the same supplies you need for soap-making can be used for these other items.

The individual chapters will give you information about the special supplies you need for each type of item you make. In this chapter, the information about supplies that follows will tell you something about the supplies that can be used for soap-making and all the other techniques in this book.

Smell Good Fragrances

As you might expect, fragrance is the most important ingredient in fragrance-crafted projects. Most of the fragrances used in this book are from fragrance oils, which are readily found in crafts stores, at bath product outlets, and from online fragrance crafting suppliers.

Fragrance oils are synthetically produced scents. Because they are much less expensive to produce than essential oils, they cost less. Fragrance oils come in a wider range of scents and blends then do essential oils, and they are safer to use with children.

Additives

Additives are things you add to soaps and bath products that supply beneficial qualities. Most are probably already in your kitchen! They add color, interest, and texture – all good qualities – to your handmade scented projects. All these additives are generally considered safe when the recommended amounts are used.

- **Oatmeal** is used whole or ground. Use only regular (long-cooking) oats.
- **Lavender buds** (dried) are relaxing and aromatic.
- **Chamomile tea** adds color and scent.
- **Candy sprinkles** are used to decorate some projects. They are made of sugar and dissolve quickly in the bath.
- **Cocoa powder** provides color and a nice chocolate scent.
- **Honey**, nature's ultimate beauty product, is made by bees from the collected nectar of flowers. It contains vital vitamins and minerals, cleans and protects the skin, and seals in moisture, leaving the skin soft and smooth.
- **Glycerin** is an odorless, thick, sticky liquid that is a by-product of commercial soapmaking. It is readily absorbed into the skin and moisturizes it, leaving skin feeling smooth and silky.
- **Powdered milk** is added to soap and salt blends to soften skin.
- **Sponge pieces** provide extra scrubbing power.
- **Small toys** make treasured surprises. Make sure they do not have any sharp pieces or edges that can scratch.
- **Unflavored gelatin powder** thickens liquid soap to make jellied soap.
- **Vitamin E** is a natural preservative that makes soap stay fresh longer and provides extra healing benefits. Simply cut or pierce the capsule and squeeze out the oil.

Kitchen Additives

Use only small amounts of these additives in your soap – they can make soap unpleasantly abrasive if you use too much. A good ratio is 1/2 to 1 teaspoon of additive in 1 cup of melted soap.

Coffee (freshly ground)	Cornmeal	Dried lemon peel	Green tea
Ground almonds	Peppermint leaves	Poppy seeds	

HELPFUL HINTS FOR USING ADDITIVES:

- **Not Too Much!** Adding too much of an additive may soften your soap or make it scratchy and uncomfortable to use. Follow the recipe and use **only** the recommend amount.

These scents are proven winners with children.

CITRUS SCENTS
Lemon	Lime
Mandarin	Orange
Pink grapefruit	Tangerine

MINTY SCENTS
Citronella	Peppermint
Spearmint	

BERRY SCENTS
Blackberry	Blueberry
Raspberry	
Strawberry	

FRUITY SCENTS
Green apple	Kiwi
Peach	Pear
Watermelon	

TROPICAL SCENTS
Coconut	Mango
Pineapple	

FLORAL SCENTS
Jasmine	Lavender
Lilac	Rose
Violet	

FRESH SCENTS
Baby Powder	Cucumber
Rain	

YUMMY SCENTS
Bubble gum	Chocolate
Cinnamon	Honey
Vanilla	

Continued on next page

Additives continued

- **Measure & Blend with Care.** Measure your additives and blend them well before adding them to melted soap. Additives like powdered milks or spices can clump up – mixing them with liquid glycerin before adding them to melted soap helps disperse them evenly.
- **Sink or Swim?** Additives such as powdered spices, seeds, or grains will either sink or float. Either is a nice effect and gives the soap a natural, whimsical look. You can add the additives to the melted soap before pouring or place them in the bottom of the soap mold before pouring in the melted soap. If you want the additives evenly suspended in the soap bar, mix the soap until it cools and thickens slightly before pouring.
- **Fresh Fruits or Vegetables in Soap.** Don't use fresh organic materials from vegetables and fruits in melt and pour soap bases. A material that is not properly dried or preserved can cause your soap to become rancid very quickly.

CAUTION!

Additives and ingredients must be used with caution – almost every additive, natural or synthetic, can trigger someone's allergy or irritate sensitive skin. If you know that a child is sensitive to any ingredient, **leave it out** of the recipe.

Here are some specifics:

- Because **essential oils** are highly concentrated and potent substances, I recommend they not be used when working with children.
- Avoid using soaps with **abrasive fillers** such as dried herbs or seeds on the face. Use them for smoothing rough spots such as elbows, knees, and hands.
- For safety, use only the natural additives suggested. If you would like to explore this area further, there are many books available to educate you about safe materials to use.
- Use only **herbs and flowers** that are clean and free of insecticides and chemicals. Sprayed plants can irritate your skin. I prefer to use plants that I have grown myself. When that's not possible, I purchase botanicals from a natural food store or fresh from the market and dry them myself.
- **Don't use** dried botanicals produced for potpourri or dried flower arranging. They are not required to be food safe and may contain harmful dyes or chemicals.
- **Almonds and cocoa powder** may produce reactions in people allergic to chocolate or nuts.
- **Honey and beeswax** may cause a reaction in people allergic to pollen. **Do not** put honey in fragrance products that will be used with infants.
- Avoid using crafted products with glitter around the eyes.
- **Small toys** are a choking hazard for children under three years of age.

SIMPLE COLOR MIXING

Children have lots of fun experimenting with mixing colors. Sometimes, however, they mix too many colors together and create muddy blends. Here are a few helpful hints for keeping colors true:

- **Primary Colors** are red, blue, and yellow.
- **Secondary Colors** are mixes of primary colors:
  Yellow + blue = green
  Red + blue = purple
  Red + yellow = orange
- **Intermediate Colors** are mixes of a primary color and a secondary color.
  Lime green = yellow + green
- **Complementary Colors** are colors that are across from one another on the color wheel.
  Red is the complement of green.
  Purple is the complement of yellow.
  Blue is the complement of orange.

When you mix a color with its complement, the result is a dulled or muted color that's less intense. Some examples:
Dusty plum = Purple + a touch of its complement, yellow
Golden ocher = Yellow + a touch of its complement, purple
Moss green = Green + a touch of its complement, red

- **Shades** are created by adding black (which darkens) or white (which brightens) to colors.

Groovy Colors

Use only colorants recommended for soapmaking – you can find them in the fragrance-crafting department of your local craft store or from soapmaking suppliers. These cosmetic grade colorants create true, clean colors and are excellent for blending and creating different hues. The liquid colors come in red, blue, yellow, orange, green, white, and black.

Food coloring is not suitable for soap recipes – the color quickly fades. It also is not suitable for bath oils, as the dye doesn't mix with oil and just sits on top as floating beads of concentrated color. You can, however, use small amounts of food coloring to color bath salts and bath fizzy products.

Lipstick is used for coloring lip balms. You can use inexpensive lipstick (the kind you find at dollar and discount stores).

For a sparkling effect, use cosmetic grade glitters. (They are a favorite with children.) Make sure you use *only* glitters that are sold for soapmaking; other glitters can be scratchy and may irritate sensitive skin.

Equipment

The basic tools and equipment for creating melt and pour soaps and bath products are standard kitchen items you possibly already own.

If you clean glass and metal tools thoroughly after using them for fragrance crafting, they can be returned to the kitchen for food preparation. Plastic and wood items used for fragrance crafting should not be used for food. It's a good idea to label them "For Fragrance Crafting Only" with a permanent marker to avoid mix-ups.

Here are the items you need:

Glass measuring cups - 1-cup, 2-cup, and 4-cup heat resistant measuring cups are the main containers for melting soap bases in the microwave or with the stovetop double boiler method.

Measuring spoons - A set of good metal or plastic ones for measuring additives.

Glass droppers - You need at least three glass droppers for measuring fragrance oils. Do not use plastic droppers. Many fragrance oils come with droppers – check the bottles before purchasing additional droppers.

Mixing spoons - Metal or wooden kitchen spoons are needed for mixing ingredients. The metal spoons will not transfer fragrances, so the spoons are safe for food use after cleaning. If you use wooden spoons, clearly label them for "For Fragrance Crafting Only" and don't use them to prepare food. (Wood retains scents and transfers them to food.)

Large saucepan - For the stovetop method of melting soap, you need a large metal saucepan. (Any metal is fine.) The pan is used to hold water; a glass measuring cup placed inside makes a double boiler for melting soap bases.

Paper cups - Small paper cups are handy for holding pre-measured additives and to use as equal size risers for tray molds that do not sit level.

Knife - A knife is needed to cut soap bases into smaller pieces for melting and to slice finished molded soaps. I use inexpensive paring knives that aren't very sharp for children to use. An adult can slice loaf soaps using a larger butcher knife.

Wax paper - Use wax paper to protect your work area when pouring and creating soaps and fragrance crafts.

Cutting board - Use a wooden cutting board for cutting soap to protect your countertop.

Water mister - You need a water mister for spraying a fine mist when making the bath fizzies.

Clean jars with lids - Use them for bath salts.

Glass bowls - Use them for mixing ingredients. It's good to have a variety of different sizes on hand.

Electric frying pan - This is handy for melting the balms and soap bases. Always use another container, such as a foil dish or glass bowl, in a water bath to melt the soap or balm ingredients.

Zipper-top plastic bags - Use these for mixing bath salts, powders, and balms (especially helpful when working with a large group of children).

THE SCIENCE OF SOAP

Soap is made of tiny molecules. One end of the molecule is attracted to water, and the other end to oil. When you bathe in soapy water, the oily dirt gets stuck to one end of the soap molecule while the other end of the molecule is stuck to the water. The soap carries the oil from your skin, leaving you squeaky clean.

Sensational Suds
Making Your Own Melt & Pour Soap

Get ready to create brilliant bars of soap for tons of bubbles
and squeaky-clean fun!

WHAT YOU NEED

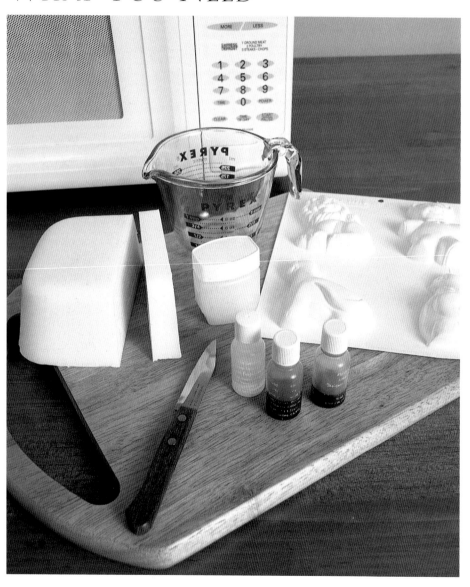

Soap Bases

The best melt and pour soap bases to use with children are clear glycerin and whitened glycerin bases. These soaps have a low melting point (between 135 and 145 degrees F.). A low melting point allows the children to participate with adult supervision and helps minimize the danger of burns. The soap is gentle enough for all skin types and has little scent, so it's ready for your own fragrance blends.

Melt and pour glycerin soap bases are available with added ingredients such as goat's milk, coconut oil, olive oil, and vitamin E. These are also excellent choices.

Pre-colored soap bases are also available in a wide range of colors, including bright fluorescents that are very popular with children.

Colorants

Use **only** colorants recommended for soapmaking, which are available at crafts stores and from soapmaking suppliers. For more information, read the "About Your Supplies" section of this book.

Fragrance

Use fragrance oils in the amounts recommended. For more information about fragrance oils and selecting scents, see the "About Your Supplies" section of this book.

 Additives

Use recommended additives in the amounts listed in the recipes for reliable results. More information about additives is included in the "About Your Supplies" section, along with cautions and tips.

 Molds

A variety of molds can be used for soaps. Here are the ones I recommend:

- **Plastic soap molds** are overall the best and safest for soapmaking with children. Their deep, clean, smooth contours allow you to create professional looking bars safely, and they are easy to unmold. Soap molds are available as individual shapes or in trays of fancy motifs. They are designed to last for a long time with repeated moldings. Large loaf soap molds are also available in a variety of sizes and shapes.

- **Tube molds** are available in basic shapes (circle, star, heart, and oval) and in motif shapes (butterfly). An advantage of a tube mold, which is vertical, over a loaf mold, which is horizontal, is that you can pour only one, two, or three inches of soap rather than filling up the entire mold. This is a great way to use up small bits of soap and make smaller batches.

- **Plastic food containers**, such as small sandwich or storage containers, with no design on the inside bottom and with nice rounded corners can be used as soap molds or containers for liquid soap projects. Choose plastic containers that are dishwasher safe. The high temperature of melted soap can cause some plastic containers – particularly disposable containers like the ones used for takeout food – to melt and collapse, spilling the hot soap.

- **Foil containers** can also be used as soap molds.

HELPFUL HINTS FOR MOLDED SOAPS

- **Don't over-heat** the soap base. Most molds can tolerate temperatures of 135 to 145 degrees F. Over-heated soap can warp even the best soap molds.

- **Always stir** the soap to help cool it down before pouring it in the mold. (This also makes the soap much safer for the children to use.)

- Release soap from tray molds by using gentle thumb pressure on the back of the mold. You can easily damage molds with improper handling.

- If you find it hard to release the soap from the mold, place the mold in the freezer for 10 minutes, then try again.

 Equipment

Cutting board on which to slice soaps
Knife for slicing soaps
Heat-resistant glass measuring cups - 2 cup and 4 cup sizes, for measuring and melting
Petroleum jelly to use as a mold release. Rub it over the inside of the mold before pouring in the melted soap base. The soap will release without sticking and the petroleum jelly won't leave a sticky residue on the soap.

WORKING WITH TUBE MOLDS

- Rub the insides of plastic and metal tube molds with a thin layer of petroleum jelly to aid in releasing the hardened soap.

- You must prepare a tube mold each and every time you pour in soap. Failing to prepare the mold, even if it comes with a cap on the bottom, will result in soap leaking out of the mold and all over your work area. To prepare a mold, place four layers of plastic wrap on the bottom of the tube mold and attach with a rubber band. Pour in 1/2" of melted soap to create a seal at the base of the mold. Let harden. After this soap plug has hardened, pour the melted soap in the mold. It won't leak.

- Let the soap cool and harden completely before attempting to push it out of the mold. *Tip:* Smaller tube molds work especially well for pushing out hardened soap from a larger tube mold. *TIP:* To prevent damage to the soap, always place a crumpled paper towel in the mold before pushing out the soap.

- The smallest molds are the hardest to release. To release soap from smaller molds, place a piece of crumpled paper towel or a coin on the soap. Use a wooden dowel or unsharpened pencil to push out the hardened soap. **Never** use a knife, fork, or other sharp utensil to push out the soap – you could injure yourself or damage the soap. *Tip:* For easier releasing, place the tube mold in the refrigerator for 10 minutes; the soap should come out easily.

- Use a knife to slice tube-molded soaps into bars. Soap made in smaller molds can be sliced 1/2" thick. Soap made in medium and large molds should be cut 3/4" to 1" thick.

HOW TO MAKE SOAP
Step-by-Step Melt and Pour Soapmaking

Julia helped me make this soap.

1. Prepare the mold by rubbing a thin layer of petroleum jelly over the inside surfaces. The petroleum jelly is a mold release – it helps the soap come out the mold easily.

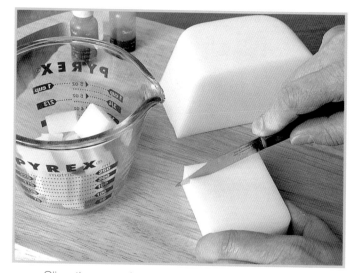

2. Slice the soap base into small pieces for quick, easy melting. Place the soap in a heat-resistant glass measuring cup. To melt one cup of soap pieces, microwave for approximately 30 seconds on high. (Melting time depends on the amount of soap and the type of soap.) Remove the cup and mix the soap, then place back in the microwave in 15-second intervals until melted. (Melting in short intervals will prevent the soap from boiling over the cup and making a mess.) Remove from the microwave and stir lightly to completely melt the remaining soap pieces.

Option: Melt the soap in a double boiler on the stove. Adjust the heat to keep the soap at a constant liquid point. **Do not** let the soap heat for more than 10 minutes.

HELPFUL HINTS FOR SUCCESSFUL SOAPMAKING

- **Do not** leave the mixing spoon in the soap while heating in the microwave or when melting on the stovetop.
- If your soap starts to solidify while you're mixing in the colorants and fragrance, gently reheat it to re-melt it.
- Re-melting won't harm the soap. If you melt too much soap for your chosen mold, just pour what's left over in a spare mold or plastic container. Release and re-melt for another project. *Tip:* Always have an extra mold on hand for leftover melted soap.

- When cleaning up, **don't** put your measuring cups or spoons in the dishwasher. Melt and pour soap bases are designed to make lots of luxurious bubbles, and the soap left on the equipment could foam and cause the dishwasher to leak. Roll up your sleeves and wash the few pieces of equipment by hand.
- Soap is meant to dissolve in water, so keep finished soap bars high and dry between uses by storing it on a soap dish with drainage.

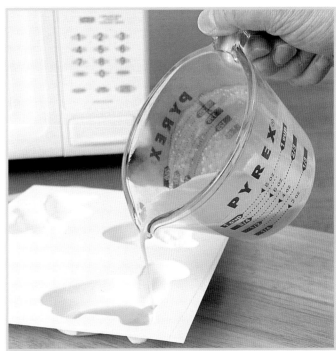

3. Immediately add any additives or coloring (specified by the recipe you're using) to the melted soap and stir gently to mix. Add the drops of fragrance oil until desired level of fragrance is achieved.

4. Pour the soap in the mold. If you have melted soap left over, pour it in a mold or a plastic container and let harden. (You can always re-melt it.)

SOAP-
MAKING
HISTORY

Historians
believe soap was
made in prehistoric times.
They think people discovered
this slippery substance that
created bubbles while cooking
over open pits when they
observed what happened
when fat and ashes
combined.

5. Let the soap cool and harden completely, then remove from the mold. The soap will pop out easily when completely set. For a fast set, allow the soap to set in the refrigerator until cooled.

Bright Fish Soaps

This is basic molded clear glycerin soap with three cool technique variations!
For one technique, colors are swirled together to make Marbled Fish. Another adds
plastic suction cups during molding so the finished soap will stick to the wall.
The third adds glitter to the molded soap.

WHAT YOU NEED

Makes four fish soaps

Soap base: 4 oz. melted clear glycerin soap base

Fragrance oil: 15 drops rain

Colors: Blue, green

Mold: Fish tray mold

HOW TO MAKE THEM

Marbled Fish

Use this technique to make soap with a marbled appearance.

1. Melt two different colors of soap at the same time. Add colorant and fragrance oil.
2. Let them cool and thicken slightly.
3. Pour the two colors of melted soap in the mold at the same time and let them gently swirl together, creating a blended marbled effect.

Stick 'em Up Fish

This is a great way to keep the soap out of the water!

1. Remove the metal hanger from a 1-3/8" plastic suction cup.
2. Melt the soap. Add colorant and fragrance oil. Pour in the mold.
3. Place two wooden craft sticks across the opening and use them to hold the suction cup in the melted soap without sinking to the bottom. Let the soap cool.
4. Remove from the mold. Use the suction cup to stick the soap to the bathroom wall.

Glitter Fish

This makes the fish soap much more glittery than adding the glitter to the melted soap.

1. Melt the soap. Add colorant and fragrance oil. Pour in the mold. Let cool.
2. Remove from the mold.
3. Use a clean, dry paint brush to brush iridescent glitter on the fish.

PACKAGING

1. Place a piece of decorative paper on a piece of thin cardboard.
2. Arrange the fish on the decorative paper.
3. Cut a colored piece of card stock with decorative edge scissors. Place under the cardboard.
4. Wrap the fish soap and paper base with clear cellophane. Secure at the back with clear tape.
5. Accent the package with trim or ribbon. Add a tag made with bubble paper and a fish sticker. ❏

Pastel Sea Soap

This basic soap shows what the soap looks like when you use whitened soap base –
you get beautiful, soft-colored bars!

WHAT YOU NEED

Makes three sea soaps

Soap base: 4 oz. melted whitened glycerin soap base

Fragrance oil: 10 drops mango, 6 drops coconut

Colors: 1 drop blue (for light blue), 1 drop blue + two drops red (for lavender), 1 drop red + 3 drops yellow (for coral)

Mold: Sea life tray mold

PACKAGING

Paper door hangers are used to make these clever fold-over packages.

1. Decorate the hanger and the tag piece with the bubble paper technique. (See "Making Bubble Paper" in the packaging section at the end of the book.)

2. Place the wrapped soap in a cellophane bag with paper shreds. Fold over the top of the bag and tape to close.

3. Fold the door hanger in half. Place the bagged soap behind the window. Tape in place.

4. Decorate the tag with a fish sticker. Tie to the top with white paper ribbon. ❏

Crayon Soaps

These are fun soaps that don't color anything. (You can load them up with colorant if you wish to make them really colorful, but beware – some colorants may color the kids and the bathtub and not wash off. To avoid this, use only universal cosmetic colorants.)

WHAT YOU NEED

Makes 4 crayon soaps

Soap base: 8 oz. melted clear glycerin soap base

Colors & fragrance oils:

For blue crayon - 2 drops blue, 6 drops peppermint

For red crayon - 2 drops red, 8 drops raspberry

For yellow crayon - 4 drops yellow, 8 drops mango

For green crayon - 3 drops yellow + 1 drop blue, 8 drops lime

Molds: Prepared 1" round tube mold, one for each color

PACKAGING

1. Release the soap from the mold. Use a knife to carve one end of each "crayon" to a point.

2. On a 3" x 3" piece of tan paper, spell the crayon color's name with alphabet stickers. Add squiggly borders with a black felt-tip pen.

3. Wrap the label around the crayon. Hold in place with a piece of tape.

4. Place the soap crayons in a cellophane bag. Accent with a bright ribbon and a paper crayon tag. ❑

Confetti Hearts Soap

WHAT YOU NEED

Makes six 1" thick soap slices

Soap base: 8 oz. melted whitened glycerin soap base

Fragrance oil: 20 drops blackberry

Additives: Blue, pink, and purple clear soap cubes – enough to fill the tube mold (You can find these already made and in packages; or you can make your own by molding soaps in a shallow mold and cutting into cube.)

Mold: Prepared 3" heart tube mold

HOW TO MAKE THEM

1. Fill the mold with clear soap cubes.

2. Melt the whitened soap base. Add fragrance oil. Pour into the mold around the colored soap cubes. Let harden.

3. Unmold and slice.

PACKAGING

1. Cut a 14" x 14" piece of clear cellophane.

2. Place soap in center. Gather cellophane around soap and tie at the top with white paper ribbon.

3. Curl the ribbon with the scissors blade. Glue on a heart charm to finish.

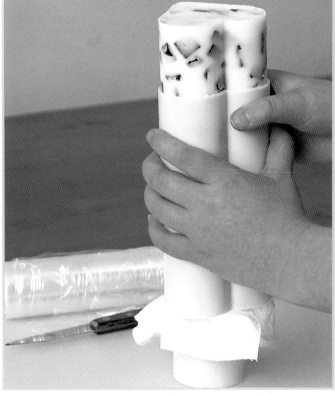

Pushing the soap from the mold. (Children can do this!)

Slicing the soap with a knife.

This jewel-studded soap is fun to slice – slicing reveals the bright soap pieces inside. Older children can cut the soap cubes or you can purchase already-cut colored soap cubes in the fragrance-crafting departments of crafts stores.

To make your own soap cubes, pour melted, colored, clear soap in rectangle soap molds or plastic containers. Let harden. Remove the soap from the mold and cut into 1/2" cubes.

Pie Soaps

This is a great soap to do with children – there's lots they can do. They can slice the tube soap, grate the white soap, and assemble the pie before the clear soap is poured over the top.

I've included two variations of the same basic recipe – Cherry Pie Soap and Banana Cream Pie Soap. It's hard to find cherry and banana fragrance oils, so blends of berry and tropical fragrance oils were used to create the scents. Each makes one pie soap that can be cut into four wedges.

WHAT YOU NEED

For Cherry Pie Soap

Soap bases:

1 tube of red soap – make this by molding 2 oz. clear soap base and 3 drops red colorant in a 1" round tube mold

1/2 cup grated white soap

4 oz. clear melted soap

Fragrance oils: 10 drops strawberry, 8 drops raspberry

Mold: 5" diameter foil pie plate

For Banana Cream Pie Soap

Soap base:

1 tube of yellow soap – make this by molding 2 oz. whitened soap base and 4 drops yellow colorant in a 1" round tube mold

1/2 cup grated white soap

4 oz. clear melted soap

Fragrance oils: 10 drops pineapple, 8 drops coconut

Mold: 5" diameter foil pie plate

HOW TO MAKE THEM

1. Slice the tube soap into 1/4" thick slices. Place in the pie plate. Save a slice for the top of the pie.
2. Place the grated white soap over the slices.
3. Add the fragrance oils to the melted clear soap base and pour in the pie plate over the slices and grated soap. Place the saved soap slice to the middle of the pie. Let set. Cut in wedges.

PACKAGING

1. Cut a piece of clear cellophane 12" x 12".
2. Place the soap wedge on the cellophane. Gather the cellophane around the soap and tie with a strip of gingham fabric.
3. Use a pie-shaped paper tag and artificial fruit for accents.
   ❏

23

Cool Two-Toned Soaps

These two-toned soaps are created when a florescent colored soap base is poured into a soap mold with a deep embossed motif and a contrasting colored soap poured on top. This results in a bar with a well-defined colored motif.

Don't wait too long to pour in the second color, or the two layers will not stick together. Use your favorite fragrances to scent these bright bars. They are a great and inexpensive project to make at a party. Packaged in bright paper bags with stickers, they're a great party favor, too.

PACKAGING

1. Wrap the soaps in cellophane.

2. Trim the tops of colored paper bags with decorative edge scissors. Fill the bags with soaps, fold over the tops of the bags, and staple to hold.

3. Glue a ribbon bow in a bright color and a colorful eraser over the staple on each bag. Stickers add the finishing touch. ❏

WHY ARE BUBBLES ROUND?

A bubble is a soapy film that holds air, and bubbles are round because the round (or sphere) shape is the most efficient shape that the soapy film can take - it takes up the least amount of surface area. A square or pyramid shape, for example, would take up more surface area, and nature takes the most efficient path.

Honey ☆ Oatmeal Soap

These flower soaps have added honey and oatmeal for a gentle scrubbing soap
that smells fantastic!

WHAT YOU NEED

Makes two blossom bars

Soap base: 6 oz. whitened glycerin soap base

Fragrance oil: 6 drops honey

Colors: 2 drops yellow

Additives: 1 teaspoon honey, 1/2 teaspoon whole oats

Mold: Blossom motif soap mold

PACKAGING

1. Place a happy face eraser on the soap before wrapping in plastic wrap.

2. Use the soap mold as a pattern for a flower-shaped paper label and cut out so it's slightly smaller than the soap. Use a happy face sticker at the center of the label.

3. Tape the label to the back of the bar. ❏

Peter Rabbit Soap

Rabbit soaps are a perfect way to welcome spring. Chamomile is added for its gentle relaxing and calming effects – just what a startled bunny needs after raiding a garden! Dried chamomile is sold as a tea – find it in the tea sections of grocery and health food stores.

WHAT YOU NEED

Makes two bars

Soap base: 6 oz. whitened glycerin soap base

Fragrance oil: 6 drops honey

Color: 2 drops yellow

Additives: 1 teaspoon honey, 1/2 teaspoon dried chamomile

Mold: Bunny motif soap mold

PACKAGING

1. Wrap the soap in plastic wrap.

2. Tape a few silk flowers to the back of the bar so it looks like the bunny is holding a bouquet of flowers.

3. Place the bar in a cellophane bag with paper shreds. Finish with a raffia bow and a flower. ❏

Cookie Cutter Stacked Soaps
Using Soap Sheets

These soaps are made from stacks of
colored soap pieces that are cut out from soap
sheets with cookie cutters. You can make the soap
sheets ahead of time and have them ready for
children to stack and decorate. Soap sheets
are a particularly good project for young children
because there is no hot, melted soap to
worry about.

HOW TO MAKE THEM

For adults – making the soap sheets:

1. Line cookie sheets with aluminum foil.
2. Melt soap base and add the fragrance oil and color of your choice.
3. Pour approximately 4 oz. melted soap on the cookie sheet. The soap will spread to a thickness of about 1/4". Let cool completely.

For children – assembling the soaps:

1. Cut out shapes with cookie cutters.
2. To stick the sheets together, use a hair dryer to slightly melt the top of a soap sheet shape before placing another on top. *Option:* Melt some clear glycerin soap base. Pour a small amount on a soap shape, then place the second shape on top.

Making stacked soaps from soap sheets.

SOAP SHEET IDEAS

Sunburst Soaps - Place cutout shapes one on top of the other but slightly askew for this whimsical look.

Glitter Bars - Use a clean dry brush to add a touch of glitter to the finished bars.

Heart with a Star - Use a small star cutter to create a window in the top heart shape. *Variation:* Older children could use a knife to carve their initial or another shape in a soap sheet.

PACKAGING

1. Wrap soap in plastic wrap.
2. Place in a cellophane bag and tie with a tulle bow. ❏

Lollipop Soaps

Lollipop-shaped soaps are another soap sheet project. Coating them with a sparkling soap glaze helps to hold the bar together. Be sure these delectable bars are clearly labeled "soap" before giving as a gift!

WHAT YOU NEED

Soap sheets, *see page 28 for how to make*

Knife and ruler

Hair dryer

Wooden skewers

Wax paper

For the sparkling glaze:

Soap base: 4 oz. clear glycerin soap base

Additive: 1/4 teaspoon soap glitter

Fragrance oils: your choice

Fragrance blend suggestions:

Bubble gum + spearmint

Lime + peppermint

Orange + vanilla

Green apple + honey

HOW TO MAKE THEM

1. With a knife and a ruler, cut soap sheets into strips approximately 1/2" x 12".
2. Place two contrasting colored strips together and roll into a swirled bar. *Tip:* You may need to soften the soap strips with a hair dryer to make them stick together.
3. Hold the coil together by piercing it with a wooden skewer.
4. Melt 4 oz. clear glycerin soap base.

Add 1/4 teaspoon soap glitter and some yummy fragrance oils. (See suggestions above.)

5. Dip the soap lollies in the melted soap and place on a piece of wax paper to cool.

PACKAGING

1. Wrap soap in plastic wrap.
2. Wrap an 8" x 8" piece of cellophane around the soap. Tie on a brightly colored ribbon to hold. ❏

Sponge in Soap

This soap uses a bow-shaped sponge – the kind sold for sponge painting. The built-in sponge is fun to use.

WHAT YOU NEED

Makes one bar

Soap base: 4 oz. melted whitened glycerin soap base

Colors: 4 drops yellow, 2 drops red

Fragrance oil: 10 drops peach

Additive: - Pink bow-shaped sponge

Mold: Square soap mold

HOW TO MAKE IT

1. Place the sponge in the mold.
2. Pour in the melted soap, pouring around the sponge and about 3/4 of the way up the sponge. Make sure the soap does not cover the sponge.
3. Let set. Unmold.

VARIATION

If your sponge has a cutout, pour in a second color after the first pouring has hardened to make a multi-colored bar. *See example of heart sponge soap on page 37.*

PACKAGING

1. Wrap soap in plastic.
2. Make a folded card a slightly larger than the soap. Trim three edges with decorative edge scissors. Write a message inside the card and decorate with stickers.
3. Place the soap on the card and secure with double-stick tape.
4. Put a sticker in the middle of the bow. ❏

Treasure Soap

These soap bars are always a big hit with children whether they make them as gifts or for themselves. To make a "mystery bar," use whitened soap base so the toy is hidden inside the soap bar. Using the soap, of course, reveals the "treasure." This soap works well for parties with pirate or princess themes.

WHAT YOU NEED

Makes two bars

Soap base: 2 oz. clear glycerin soap base, 4 oz. whitened glycerin soap base

Fragrance oil: 10 drops

Color: 1 to 2 drops colorant (to the white soap base)

Additives: Small toys to embed

Molds: Simple bar shapes, rectangles, or rounds (whatever holds the chosen toys best)

Optional: Soap glitter

HOW TO MAKE IT

1. Pour a small amount of clear glycerin soap in the mold. Wait a minute until a skin forms on the top. Carefully remove the skin with the point of a knife. (This removes any bubbles or foam from the top of the soap.)
2. While the soap is still liquid, add the toys *face down* to the mold. Let the soap harden.
3. Pour a second layer of soap, using a colored whitened glycerin soap base that contrasts with the color of the toy. *Option:* Add soap glitter to this layer for a sparkling effect.

PACKAGING

1. Wrap the soap in plastic.
2. Place in a cellophane bag.
3. Accent with a sheer ribbon bow and gold coin. ❏

CAUTIONS

- Use safe, soft toys – don't use anything that is sharp or has points.
- Soaps with small toys should not be given to children under three years of age.

Dipped Foam Shapes

Dipping craft foam shapes in clear melted soap base makes these bright soap shapes. They are a one-time use soap that can sit in a pretty dish next to the sink. The foam shapes can be re-used to make more soaps or for another craft project. The foam shapes also can be layered, as with the circle piece for the flower center.

These soaps harden quickly, so they can be wrapped up soon after making. This is an economical project for a large group of children – it uses little soap and the foam shapes are inexpensive.

WHAT YOU NEED

Soap base: 4 oz. melted clear glycerin soap

Fragrance oil: 10 drops (For flowers, use a floral fragrance like violet or lilac.)

Foam shapes: hands and/or flowers with or without center circles

Optional - 1/4 teaspoon soap glitter

HOW TO MAKE THEM

1. Melt soap and mix in fragrance oil and glitter, if you wish.
2. Stir the soap until it has cooled down a bit. It should be cool enough to touch, but still liquid. If the soap starts to clump and harden, place it back in the microwave for a few seconds to re-melt.
3. Let children dip the foam shapes in the soap.
4. Place the dipped shapes on a sheet of wax paper to cool. *Option:* Dip the shapes a second time for a thicker soap coating.

PACKAGING

1. While the soaps are hardening, let children decorate 3-1/2" x 8-1/2" pieces of brightly colored paper with stickers and felt pens and label their soaps with the name of the soap and instructions for use. See the box for sample instructions.
2. Place the soap shapes on the blank side of the paper and place in a cellophane bag. Tape closed. ❏

INSTRUCTIONS FOR USE

Include these instructions when you give foam shapes soaps as gifts.

For Wash your Paws! Hand-shaped Soaps:
Wash your paws with these handy-dandy soaps! Use just one to scrub away nasty germs and dirt. The soap is now used up, but keep the hand shape for crafting fun.

For Oopsie-daisy! Soaps:
Don't forget to wash your hands with these sweet scented flowers. Use just one to scrub away nasty germs and dirt. The soap is now used up, but keep the flower shape for crafting fun.

Rainbow Loaf Soap

This soap is made in a half-circle loaf mold. The soap chunks in the mold make the soap cool down and cure quickly so children can package and use the soap right away. Rainbow Soap is made in two steps.

Makes ten 1/2" soap slices

Step One - Colored Soap Chunks

WHAT YOU NEED

For the soap chunks

Blue: 4 oz. melted clear glycerin soap base, 3 drops blue colorant, 8 drops peppermint fragrance oil

Yellow: 4 oz. melted clear glycerin soap base, 5 drops yellow colorant, 10 drops lemon fragrance oil

Red: 4 oz. melted clear glycerin soap base, 3 drops red colorant, 10 drops watermelon fragrance oil

Mold: Rectangular mold that holds 1 cup

HOW TO MAKE THEM

1. Working one color at a time, melt soap base. Add colorant and fragrance oil.
2. Pour in a rectangular soap mold. Let cool.
3. Cut into 1/2" square pieces.

Step Two - Loaf Soap

WHAT YOU NEED

Soap base: 6 oz. melted clear glycerin soap base

Mold: Half-circle loaf mold

HOW TO MAKE IT

1. Place the colored soap chunks in layers in a half-circle loaf mold.
2. Pour 6 oz. melted clear glycerin soap base over the chunks and let set.
3. Slice the large bar into 1/2" slices.

PACKAGING

1. Wrap soap slices in plastic wrap.
2. Cut 1/2" wide strips of rainbow paper for labels. Write the name of the soap on the label.
3. Wrap the paper strips around the soap and tape ends together on the flat side. ❏

Scrubby Soap

The bright colored scrubby gives the color to this fun soap that has a built-in hanger to keep it handy in the shower. Scrubby soap kits are also available at crafts stores.

WHAT YOU NEED

Soap base: Clear glycerin soap base

Fragrance oil: 10 drops

Additive: Scrubby with cord

Mold: Dome soap mold

HOW TO MAKE IT

1. Push the scrubby into a dome-shaped mold, making sure the cord is at the top. Don't worry if the scrubby keeps popping out, it will stay in once you pour in the melted soap. Let harden.
2. Unmold.

PACKAGING

1. Cut an 18" x 18" piece of cellophane. Wrap around the soap.
2. Tie with a matching tulle bow.
3. Add a gift card with an acrylic charm to accent the package. ❏

Loofah Heart Soaps

WHAT YOU NEED

Makes two bars

Soap base: 4 oz. clear glycerin soap base

Color: 4 drops red

Fragrance oils: 6 drops rose, 4 drops vanilla

Additives: 2 slices of loofah sponge, each 1" thick

Molds: 2 heart-shaped soap molds

HOW TO MAKE IT

1. Soak the loofah sponges in hot water for 10 minutes.

2. Push one softened sponge in each heart-shaped mold. Let dry overnight.

3. Melt the soap base. Add colorant and fragrance oil.

4. Pour in mold. Let harden.

5. Unmold.

PACKAGING

1. Wrap the soap in pink tulle and tie with a pink tulle bow.

2. Glue on silk blossoms and an acrylic gem to accent. ❏

Pictured top right: Sponge in Soap, see page 31 for instructions on making.

Soap on a Rope

Use soft nylon cording that will not disintegrate in the bath for success with this soap tradition. The soap samples use the two-toned soap method.

Dragonfly Soap on a Rope

WHAT YOU NEED

Makes two bars

First layer - 2 oz. melted clear glycerin soap base, 2 drops green colorant

Second layer - 6 oz. melted whitened glycerin soap base, 3 drops blue colorant, 20 drops rain fragrance oil

Additive: 20" piece of soft nylon cord

Mold: Rectangle soap mold with dragonfly motif

SOAP-MAKING HISTORY

In the Middle Ages, bathing was considered dangerous and unsanitary, and soap was used only to clean clothes. It wasn't until the 17th century that cleanliness and bathing became fashionable again.

Ladybug Soap on a Rope

WHAT YOU NEED

Makes two bars

First layer - 2 oz. melted clear glycerin soap base, 2 drops red colorant

Second layer - 6 oz. melted whitened glycerin soap base, 20 drops pink grapefruit fragrance oil

Additive: 20" piece of soft nylon cord

Mold: Soap mold with ladybug motif

HOW TO MAKE THEM

1. Melt the clear soap base and add the colorant. Pour in the bottom of the mold filling only the design area. Let set.
2. Melt the whitened soap base. Add colorant if needed and fragrance oil. Pour in mold.
3. Knot the ends of a 20" piece of cord and place in the freshly poured soap. Let harden.
4. Unmold.

PACKAGING

1. Cut a 4" x 5" piece of colored card paper. Place in a cellophane bag.
2. Wrap soap in plastic. Coil and tie rope. Place in bag.
3. Tie the bag with a brightly colored ribbon. Make a card decorated with a piece of bubble paper. (See "Making Bubble Paper" in the Packaging section for instructions.)
❑

Fossil Soaps

Fossil soaps are fun to create with all your little bits of leftover soap – many different colored and scented pieces can be used for this mud-colored soap bar. The fossil imprints are made with plastic creepy-crawlies, which leave detailed impressions.

Children can use plastic knives to carve out the bugs from the finished soap and use them to decorate the packages.

Scarab Soap

WHAT YOU NEED

Makes one bar

Soap base: 4 oz. colored and scented glycerin soap scraps

Color: (if needed for the mud color) - 3-4 drops black

Fragrance oil: 10 drops vanilla

Additive: 1/2 teaspoon dried peppermint leaves or lavender buds

Mold: Rectangle soap mold lined with aluminum foil

Addition: Plastic toy bug

Other Supplies: Aluminum foil, rubber cement, plastic knife

HOW TO MAKE IT

1. Line the mold with aluminum foil. (This gives a natural stone look to the finished soap.)
2. Glue the plastic bug, right side up, in the bottom of the mold with rubber cement. (If you don't glue it, it will float to the top.)
3. Melt the soap. Add colorant, if needed, and fragrance oil.
4. Pour the soap in the mold, let harden, then release.
5. Use the plastic knife to carve out the plastic toy from the soap.

PACKAGING

1. Wrap soap in plastic.
2. Place on a bed of paper shreds in a small box.
3. Decorate the box with the plastic toy used to make the soap.
4. Use a gel pen with metallic ink to label the soap and write a message. ❏

Fossil soap By Julia

Scarab Beetle
Dicronorrhina derbyanna

SOAP-MAKING HISTORY

A soap factory, complete with bars of soap, was found in the ruins of Pompeii.

Soap Dough

This soap can be hand-molded like modeling clay. It's easy to make using an electric mixer or hand beater so you can make lots of different colors. Mixing the soap as it cools is the secret that makes this recipe work. The cornstarch keeps the soap from hardening into a solid bar; the added glycerin supplies elasticity, making a moldable dough.

Let children mold soap shapes; you can then showcase their creations by placing the shape in a mold and pouring melted clear soap base around it.

WHAT YOU NEED

Soap base: 4 oz. glycerin soap base

Fragrance oils: 10-20 drops pineapple, lilac, or strawberry

Colors: 5-6 drops yellow, blue, or red

Additives: 1/4 cup cornstarch plus extra cornstarch for mixing; 1 tablespoon liquid glycerin
Optional - Soap glitter

Other Supplies: Wax paper; electric mixer, whisk, or egg beater

HOW TO MAKE IT

1. Mix the cornstarch, liquid glycerin, fragrance oil, and colorant together in a small glass bowl.
2. Melt the soap base. Mix with the colored, scented cornstarch mixture.
3. With an electric mixer, whisk, or egg beater, mix the soap until it cools and starts to set up.
4. Turn out the soap on a piece of wax paper you have sprinkled with cornstarch.
5. Coat your hands with a small amount of cornstarch and gently knead the cooled soap until it is smooth with no hardened soap bits.
   - *If the soap starts sticking to your hands,* add a sprinkling of cornstarch to your hands and the soap.
   - *If the soap dough is very sticky,* place it on a sheet of wax paper and leave it uncovered for a day.

6. Let children mold the soap into shapes with their hands.

VARIATION

1. Place the children's molded soap creations in a soap mold.
2. Place the mold with the soap shapes in the freezer for 30 minutes. (This prevents them from melting in the next step.) Remove from freezer.
3. Pour clear melted soap over the shapes in the mold to encase the artwork. ❏

Bubble Gum Soap

These individual one-time soaps are fun to squish around while you wash your hands.
The residue they leave in the sink is nominal; they tend to dissolve quickly.

WHAT YOU NEED

Soap base: 4 oz. melted glycerin soap base

Fragrance oil: 10 drops bubble gum

Color: 4 drops red

Additives: 1/4 cup cornstarch plus extra cornstarch for mixing, 1 tablespoon liquid glycerin

Other Supplies: Wax paper; electric mixer, whisk, or egg beater

HOW TO MAKE IT

1. Mix the cornstarch, liquid glycerin, fragrance oil, and colorant together in a small glass bowl.
2. Melt the soap base. Mix with the colored, scented cornstarch mixture.
3. With an electric mixer, whisk, or egg beater, mix the soap until it cools and starts to set up.
4. Turn out the soap on a piece of wax paper you have sprinkled with cornstarch.
5. Coat your hands with a small amount of cornstarch and gently knead the cooled soap until it is smooth with no hardened soap bits.
   - *If the soap starts sticking to your hands,* add a sprinkling of cornstarch to your hands and the soap.
   - *If the soap dough is very sticky,* place it on a sheet of wax paper and leave it uncovered for a day.
6. Let children mold the soap into 1" balls.

PACKAGING

1. Wrap each soap "gumball" in a 6" x 6" piece of cellophane. Twist the ends to hold.
2. Place the wrapped soap in a labeled cellophane bag and tie closed with white paper ribbon. ❏

Kids Love Bubbles!
Making Your Own Bubble Bath
& Liquid Soap Blends

This chapter will have you making bubble baths, bubbling jellies and foaming bath oils using a ready-made liquid soap base.

WHAT YOU NEED

❀ Liquid Soap Base

Liquid glycerin soap base is a concentrated, unscented formulation for creating your own quality bubble bath blends, fragrant blowing bubbles, shampoos, and fragrant liquid hand soaps. You can find liquid glycerin soap base in the fragrance-crafting departments of crafts stores. You cannot make liquid soap by adding water to melt and pour soap – that results in a slimy mess.

Alternately, you can try a clear, unscented liquid hand soap or shampoo in the liquid recipes. Because there is such a large variety of liquid soap on the market, always test it before using with children in a large project.

❀ Additives

Additives can include glycerin, almond oil, and distilled water.

❀ Colorants & Fragrance Oils

Use the same colorants and fragrance oils for liquid soaps that are recommended for molded soaps.

❀ Tools & Equipment

Heat-resistant glass measuring cups for measuring and heating
Funnel for pouring into decorative containers
Spoon for mixing and skimming
Additions and decorations like toy bugs, for fun touches and to extend a packaging theme
Decorative containers for packaging

How to Make It

Olivia helped me make Swamp Bubbles.

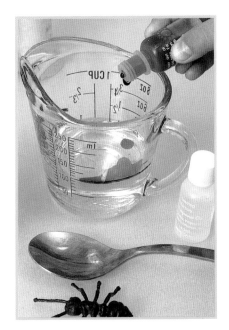

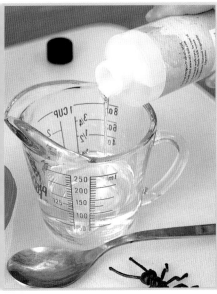

1. Measure liquid soap in a measuring cup. (Children can do this.)

2. Add additives, colorants, and fragrance oils. (Children can do this, too.) Mix gently. This step must be done before adding any other additives.

Place the mixture in the microwave and heat on high for 10 seconds. (*Option:* Place the glass measuring cup in a saucepan of water and heat on top of the stove.) Heating helps thin the mixture and expel the bubbles that were trapped when the soap was stirred. Heat very gently and slowly, in additional 10-second intervals, allowing the soap to expel the bubbles. Do not allow the mixture to boil; if you do, it will create more bubbles.

Let the mixture cool and using a spoon, skim off the expelled bubbles. If you wish a thicker consistency, add more liquid soap base at this time.

4. Add additions or decorations. (Here, it's a plastic toy, and Olivia is doing it.)

3. Pour into decorative containers. (Children can do this.)

Swamp Bubbles

This is a great bubble bath with a refreshing scent. Both boys and girls love the added creatures to play with in the tub.

To use, pour about a 1/4 cup into the running water when filling the tub – you'll get mounds of bubbles.

WHAT YOU NEED

Makes 1 cup bubble bath

Soap base: 1/2 cup liquid soap base

Fragrance oils: 10 drops spearmint, 10 drops lime

Color: 5 drops green

Additives: 1/4 cup liquid glycerin, 1/4 cup distilled water, 1 teaspoon sugar (dissolve in the distilled water)

Plastic toys: snakes, bugs, lizards, or other swamp creatures

HOW TO DO IT

Follow the basic instructions for liquid soaps. Pour the bubble bath in small food storage containers and add the plastic toys. Place lids securely on containers.

PACKAGING

1. Use tape to ensure the tops stay tightly closed.
2. Add a paper strip around the container for the label.
3. Glue a piece of decorative paper and a plastic lizard or other toy on the top. ❏

Bubbling Jelly

This bubble bath in jelly form is fun to scoop out of the jar and into the bath. It can also be placed by the sink and used as a hand wash.

WHAT YOU NEED

Makes 1 cup

Soap base: 1/2 cup liquid soap base

Fragrance oils: 10 drops raspberry, 10 drops peppermint

Color: 5 drops red

Additives: 1 pkg. unflavored gelatin powder, 1/2 cup hot water, 1/4 teaspoon soap glitter

HOW TO MAKE IT

1. Dissolve the gelatin powder in the hot water.
2. Add the fragrance oils and colorant to the liquid soap base.
3. Add glitter. Gently stir into the softened gelatin until well blended.
4. Pour into a lidded jar and set aside to cool and firm into a gel.

PACKAGING

1. Cut pink paper to fit around the jar and on top of the lid.
2. Cut strips of self-adhesive glitter paper to make a border above and below the label on the jar. Cut a circle of glitter paper with decorative edge scissors and stick on the lid.
3. Use sticker alphabet letters on the label.
4. Glue an acrylic heart charm on the lid. ❏

Foaming Honey Bath Oil

The addition of liquid honey gives extra softening and scent to this foaming bath oil. It also tints the soap a nice soft amber color. This foaming bath oil will separate in the bottle, giving a layered look. To use, shake to mix before pouring 1/4 cup into the bath.

WHAT YOU NEED

Makes 1-1/2 cups

Soap base: 1/2 cup liquid soap base

Fragrance oils: 10 drops honey, 15 drops orange

Additives: 1/2 cup almond oil, 1/2 cup honey

HOW TO MAKE IT

Follow the Basic Instructions for making bubble bath. Pour in a plastic bottle.

PACKAGING

1. Glue a simple white label to a piece of rainbow paper and wrap around the bottle.

2. Trim the edges of the label with a gold strip sticker. Decorate with pressed flower stickers and bee stickers.

3. Wrap the bottle in a 24" x 24" piece of cellophane. Tie with sheer gold ribbon. ❏

Glitter Bubbling Bath Oil

A tiny bit of soap glitter and some silk flowers dress up this pink bubble bath. Use 1/4 cup in the bath.

WHAT YOU NEED

Makes 1-1/2 cups

Soap base: 1 cup liquid soap base

Fragrance oils: 10 drops rose, 15 drops baby powder

Color: 5 drops red

Additives: 1/2 cup almond oil, 6 small pink and purple silk flowers, 1/4 teaspoon soap glitter

HOW TO MAKE IT

1. Follow the Basic Instructions for liquid soap.

2. Pour in a plastic bottle. Add the silk flowers.

PACKAGING

1. Cut pink paper to fit around the plastic bottle.

2. Use felt-tip pens to write the label.

3. Cut strips of self-adhesive silver glitter paper with decorative edge scissors and adhere to top and bottom of paper strip.

4. Tie a pink tulle bow around the neck of the bottle. ❏

Fizzing Fun!
Making Solid Fizzing Bath Salts

Solid fizzing bath salts ("bath fizzies") are a blast to use and very easy to make. Fizzies spin, bubble, and sparkle in the bath while they release wonderful scents and skin softeners. Thorough mixing of the ingredients is important to the success of the bath fizzy. The combination of baking soda and citric acid makes the fizzing action. You can demonstrate this chemical reaction to children by adding baking soda to a glass of water and citric acid to another glass of water. Nothing happens. Then mix baking soda and citric acid together before adding to a glass of water and watch the dazzling bubbling action.

WHAT YOU NEED

❀ Baking Soda (sodium bicarbonate)

This is a white powder that softens and deodorizes. It is a salt base that absorbs fragrances and releases them when it hits the warm water of the bath. When baking soda is mixed with an acid, such as citric acid, carbon dioxide is produced. (That's the fizz.) Buy baking soda at grocery stores.

❀ Citric Acid

This is made from citrus fruit, such as lemons and oranges. When mixed with baking soda, it creates the fizz. Citric acid is a great toner for your skin. Find it at health food stores and winemaking supply stores.

 Cornstarch

This is a very fine, white starchy powder made from corn. In bath fizzies, it is used as a binder and makes the mixture easier to form.

Colorants

Use liquid colorants. You can't make bright or dark colored fizzies; because of the large amount of white ingredients they all will be pale pastel hues.

Fragrances

Use fragrance oils to scent the fizzies.

Molds

Choose deep molds with large details. A mold release isn't necessary. Plastic soap molds that have deep, clean, smooth contours are great for bath fizzies. They come in individual shapes or in trays of fancy motifs.

Other Supplies & Equipment

Water mister: Use a mister to moisten the ingredients before molding.

Glass bowls: 1 small, 1 large, for mixing.

4" x 4" pieces of cardboard: for holding the fizzies as they dry. (Have lots on hand.)

BASIC BATH FIZZY RECIPE

1 cup baking soda

3/4 cup citric acid

1/4 cup cornstarch

20 drops fragrance oil

5 drops liquid colorant

Mister bottle filled with water

DIRECTIONS FOR USING A BATH FIZZY

Draw a warm bath and drop the bath fizzy in the water. Hop in and enjoy the fizzing action as it soothes your skin and releases the wonderful aromas.

Bath fizzies are easy to make and fun to use, and children can do almost all of the steps themselves.

HOW TO MAKE BATH FIZZIES

1. Put all the dry ingredients in a large glass bowl. Use your hands to break up any lumps. (Children can do this.)

2. Mix the ingredients with your hands or a wooden spoon. Mixing thoroughly at this step is one secret to perfect bath fizzies! (Children can do this.)

3. Remove approximately 1/2 cup of the mixed dry ingredients and place in the small bowl. Add the colorant(s) and fragrance oil(s) to the dry ingredients in the smaller bowl. Mix well – use the spoon to start, then mix with your hands to get the colorant(s) and fragrance oil(s) evenly distributed. Place the colored, fragrant mix back in the large bowl. Mix well. (Children can do this.)

4. Spritz the mixture lightly with a fine mist of the liquid asked for in the recipe. Do not over-mist or the mixture will start to fizz! It needs to just be damp enough to hold together. Mix well with your hands, so you can judge the dampness. If the ingredients don't hold together, mist again and continue mixing. (An adult should do this.)

5. Pack the misted mixture in a mold. (Mold release isn't necessary.) Press down hard to pack the mixture in, adding more if needed. Pack one mold at a time. (Children can do this.)

6. Place a piece of cardboard over the mold and flip over. The solid bath form will fall out on the cardboard. Be gentle! They are very fragile at this time. Place the molded bath fizzy aside and continue making more. (Children can do this.)

Leave the fizzies to dry until they are hard and solid. This can take a few hours or overnight, depending upon how much moisture is in the air.

THE SCIENCE OF THE BATH FIZZY

When sodium bicarbonate (baking soda) is mixed with citric acid, a gas (carbon dioxide) is formed that bubbles out of the water, making the fizz. A bath fizzy doesn't fizz until you get it wet.

HELPFUL HINTS

- Work quickly – the mixture can dry out and not hold together.

- If your bath fizzy breaks at any time, just re-mold.

- If your bath fizzy seems to grow and puff out, you have added too much water! Take the fizzy, place it back in the bowl, mix in some baking soda to stop the fizzing action, and re-mold.

- There is no need to wrap bath fizzies in plastic wrap before packaging.

Wake-up Sun & Dream-on Moon Bath Fizzies

The yellow sun bath fizzies, scented with invigorating lemon and peppermint are for morning baths where you want to wake up and get going. The lavender-scented blue moon bath fizzies are for relaxing evening baths.

WHAT YOU NEED

1 cup baking soda

3/4 cup citric acid

1/4 cup cornstarch

15 drops lavender fragrance, 10 drops lemon fragrance, 6 drops peppermint fragrance

4 drops blue color, 6 drops yellow color

Sun and moon molds

Water

Liquid glycerin

Mister bottle

2 glass bowls

HOW TO MAKE THEM

1. Fill the mister bottle with equal amounts of water and liquid glycerin.
2. Mix the dry ingredients.
3. Divide the dry ingredients, placing half in each of two bowls.
4. To one bowl of dry ingredients, add 4 drops blue colorant and 15 drops lavender fragrance oil. Mist and form the fizzies in a crescent moon-shaped mold.
5. To the other bowl of dry ingredients, add 6 drops yellow colorant, 10 drops lemon fragrance oil, and 6 drops peppermint fragrance oil. Mist and form the fizzies in a sun mold.

PACKAGING

1. Place blue shredded paper in a cellophane bag printed with gold stars.
2. Add one sun fizzy and one moon fizzy.
3. Tie with a sheer gold ribbon to close. ❏

Bath Bon-Bons

These yummy bath fizzies are fun for children to decorate by dipping into melted soap and then into candy sprinkles. They are formed with a melon baller and the recipe makes lots!

To use, add three or four bon-bons to a bath. (The colorful candy sprinkles are just sugar and dissolve quickly.)

WHAT YOU NEED

For the fizzies

1 cup baking soda

3/4 cup citric acid

1/4 cup cornstarch

10 drops peppermint fragrance oil

10 drops honey fragrance oil

Melon baller

Mister bottle filled with water

For dipping

4 oz. whitened glycerin soap base

5 drops red colorant

Candy sprinkles

Several shallow dishes

Wax paper

HOW TO MAKE THEM

1. Mix the dry ingredients.
2. Add fragrance oils and mix thoroughly.
3. Mist with water to dampen.
4. Using a melon baller as a mold, make small half-circle shaped fizzies. Let fizzies harden completely.
5. Melt the soap base and add the colorant. Stir the melted soap until cool enough to touch but still liquid. Place candy sprinkles in shallow dishes.
6. Dip each fizzy in melted soap, then in candy sprinkles. Place on wax

paper. Let the soap completely cool and harden.

PACKAGING

1. Place in paper candy cups in a candy box with a clear window on shreds of iridescent paper shreds.
2. Hold the box closed with gold elastic cord.
3. Be sure to label the box clearly – these fizzies smell and look good enough to eat. ❏

55

Dinosaur Egg Surprise Fizzies

Each of these egg-shaped bath fizzies has a small plastic toy dinosaur inside that "hatches" as the fizzy dissolves in the bath. Large plastic Easter eggs make great molds for this project, and making the fizzies mixture in two different colors gives a fun, two-toned look to the eggs.

DINOSAUR EGG
BATH FIZZY

Place a dinosaur egg in your
bath to hatch a fragrant,
bubbling pool of fun!
Who will you find in your egg?

WHAT YOU NEED

1 cup baking soda

3/4 cup citric acid

1/4 cup cornstarch

10 drops orange fragrance oil

10 drops cinnamon fragrance oil

4 drops red color

4 drops blue color

Mister bottle filled with water

Oval or egg-shape mold

Small plastic dinosaur toys - 1 per egg

2 glass bowls

HOW TO MAKE THEM

1. Mix the dry ingredients.
2. Divide the dry ingredients, placing half in each of two bowls.
3. To one bowl of dry ingredients, add the blue colorant and the cinnamon fragrance oil.
4. To the other bowl, add the red colorant and orange fragrance oil.
5. Mist both bowls with water and mix completely.
6. Pack a little of each color mixture in the mold. Place the plastic toy in the mold, and fill the mold to the top, packing tightly.
7. Release from the mold and let dry.

PACKAGING

1. Place the eggs in a tan paperboard box on a bed of wooden excelsior.
2. Add some plastic greenery and a small plastic dinosaur.
3. Type and print a label on a computer and glue inside the box lid.
4. Decorate the box with dinosaur stickers or plastic buttons. ❏

Snowball Fizzies

These bath fizzies don't require a mold – they are hand-formed just like snowballs. Making them is a perfect activity for children who live in warm climates and don't get to experience the real thing! The scents are invigorating and refreshing, and the extra sparkle makes the bath water shimmer.

WHAT YOU NEED

1 cup baking soda

3/4 cup citric acid

1/4 cup cornstarch

5 drops peppermint fragrance oil

15 drops rain fragrance oil

1 teaspoon soap glitter or cosmetic grade glitter

Mister bottle filled with water

Wax paper

HOW TO MAKE THEM

1. Mix the dry ingredients.
2. Add fragrance oils and glitter and mix thoroughly.
3. Mist with water to dampen.
4. Scoop up small handfuls of the damp mixture and press with your hands to make firm, rounded shapes. Place on wax paper and let dry completely.

PACKAGING

1. Place iridescent paper shreds in a cellophane bag.
2. Add the dry bath fizzies.
3. Accent the bag with a piece of white star garland and a small snowman ornament. ❏

Inset photo at left: Hand-forming Bath Snowballs.

Bath Biscuits

No molds or special colorants are needed to form these yummy scented bath biscuits. It's an easy, economical project for a large group.

WHAT YOU NEED

1 cup baking soda

3/4 cup citric acid

1/4 cup cornstarch

3 teaspoons cocoa powder

10 drops chocolate fragrance oil

10 drops vanilla fragrance oil

Mister bottle filled with water

Candy sprinkles

Wax paper

HOW TO MAKE THEM

1. Mix the dry ingredients, including the cocoa powder.
2. Add fragrance oils and mix thoroughly.
3. Mist with water to dampen.

SOME INTERESTING USES OF FRAGRANCE

Vanilla scent is used to relax patients undergoing imaging scans at medical clinics.

The smell of freshly baked bread has been re-created as a room spray to help sell houses.

4. Scoop up enough of the mixture to make 2" balls. Place on wax paper and press to form the cookie shape. Add some candy sprinkles on top and push in to hold. Let dry and harden before moving.

PACKAGING

1. Place Bath Biscuits on a bed of paper shreds in a cardboard box with a window.
2. Decorate the front of the package with a torn fabric bow, a large button, and alphabet stickers (for the label). Be sure the recipient understands they are NOT food. ❑

Salty Soaks!
Making Your Own Bath Salts

Bath salts are incredibly easy to create, making them ideal for children to make. Measuring and counting the fragrance and coloring drops can be educational and fun. The ingredients for bath salts can be found at supermarkets and health food stores, and bath salts can be produced at a fraction of the cost of store-bought salts. The scents are soothing, and Epsom salts relax you and heal your skin.

WHAT YOU NEED

 Epsom Salts

Epsom salts are the base for the bath salts. They are a fine white mineral (magnesium sulfate) in crystal form that soothes sore muscles in the bath. Epsom salts easily disperse in water.

 Salt

Coarse salt, rock salt, and sea salt are sodium chloride – the kind of salt you sprinkle on food can be used instead of Epsom salts as the base for your bath salts. Salts neutralize the oils on your skin so the fragrance will cling and make your skin smell nice. Salt is also very soothing and healing to add to your bath.

Other Supplies & Equipment

Liquid colorants for tinting
Fragrance oil for scenting
Jar with a lid for mixing
Spoons for moving salts into the jar and the decorative containers
Measuring cups for measuring the salts
Decorative containers for packaging

Directions for Using Bath Salts

Draw a warm bath and add 1/4 cup of the fragrant salts to the running water. Hop in and relax, inhaling deeply to experience the soothing qualities of the delightful aromas.

How to Make Them, Step by Step

1. Measure the amount of salts called for in the recipe into a clean jar.

2. Add fragrance oils and colorants.

3. Place the lid on the jar and be sure it is on tight. Mix the salts by shaking the jar.

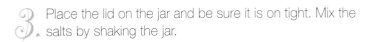

4. Spoon the finished salts into decorative containers.

Fruity Rainbow Bath Salts

These colored salts are scented with fruit fragrances. Make them in your favorite colors or choose colors to coordinate with the colors of your bathroom.

FRAGRANCE CRAFTING HISTORY

Ancient Egyptians regarded perfumed products as the "sweat of the gods." Their scent blends included almonds, roses, frankincense, and myrrh. So sophisticated were their blends that ointments discovered in Tutankhamen's tomb in 1922 were still fragrant

WHAT YOU NEED

1-1/4 cups rock or coarse salt

5 glass jars with lids

Plastic tube containers for packaging

Optional: Epsom salts

For red layer

3 drops red color

10 drops watermelon fragrance oil

For yellow layer

5 drops yellow color

10 drops pear fragrance oil

For green layer

3 drops green color

10 drops kiwi fragrance oil

For blue layer

3 drops blue color

10 drops blueberry fragrance oil

For purple layer

2 drops red color

1 drop blue color

10 drops blackberry fragrance oil

HOW TO MAKE THEM

1. Place 1/4 cup of coarse or rock salt in each of five jars. Reserve the Epsom salts. (See below.)
2. To each jar, add colorant and fragrance oil to make one color and scent combination. Place lids on jars and shake to blend in the color and scent.
3. Spoon layers of different colors into plastic tubes. *Option:* For variety, spoon a white Epsom salts layer between the colored layers.
4. Add a simple label and brightly colored happy face erasers to the tops of the containers. ❑

Chocolate Milk Bath

This is a favorite bath salt that gives a soothing, silky bath with the luscious aroma of chocolate. To use, spoon 1/4 cup of the salts into the bath.

WHAT YOU NEED

1/2 cup powdered milk

1 cup Epsom salts

2 teaspoons cocoa powder

10 drops chocolate fragrance oil

20 drops vanilla fragrance oil

Glass jar with lid

HOW TO MAKE THEM

1. Place dry ingredients in the jar.
2. Add fragrance oils and shake to mix.

PACKAGING

1. Place the finished salts in a plastic jar.
2. Decorate with decorative paper and label with alphabet stickers.
3. Accent the lid with a torn strip of fabric and a button. ❏

Candy Cane Bath Salts

Use these for holiday gift-giving.

WHAT YOU NEED

Epsom salts
Red color
Cinnamon fragrance oil
Peppermint fragrance oil
2 jars with lids

HOW TO MAKE THEM

1. Place about one third of the Epsom salts in a jar. Add peppermint fragrance oil and shake to mix.
2. Place remaining Epsom salts in the other jar. Add red colorant and cinnamon fragrance oil. Shake to mix.

PACKAGING

1. Spoon into plastic tubes in layers for the candy cane look.
2. Hand letter a sticky label for each tube.
3. Decorate with curling ribbon and a Santa eraser. ❏

Better-than-Good Balms!
Making Lip Gloss, Solid Perfume & Lotions

Balms are children's favorite projects to make and use! One balm base can be used to make lip balm, solid perfume, glitter stick, and the bugs-be-gone lotion bar. Balms are very economical to make, as very little base is needed to fill the containers.

WHAT YOU NEED

❀ Balm Base Ingredients

The balm base is almond oil and beeswax melted together. The consistency of the balm is determined by amount of beeswax you use. For a softer balm, use less; for a firmer balm, use more. Different additives are used to make different products.

Almond Oil: This light, odorless oil is pressed from the kernel (seed) of the almond. Almond oil is easily absorbed into the skin. It protects and nourishes skin and contains vitamin E, which keeps it fresh. Sweet almond oil is basically the same product, but is much more expensive.
Options: Safflower and sunflower oils can also be used in the recipes. If you use them, add three capsules of vitamin E to each cup of oil to keep them fresher longer.

Beeswax: White beeswax is best for creating your base – the impurities have been filtered out but it still has the honey aroma. If you can't find white beeswax, use amber-hued natural beeswax. (Be aware it may affect the color of your finished project.) Beeswax in pellet form is the easiest to use, but beeswax sheets or blocks also can be melted and used.

❀ Flavoring

When making lip gloss, use a flavoring rather than a fragrance. Oil-based flavorings used in candy making are the best, but you can also use flavor extracts used in cooking. Small amounts of chocolate or candy powder can be used as flavorings for lip balm.

❀ Other Supplies & Equipment

Measuring spoons for measuring ingredients
Glass bowl for holding the hot water
Kettle for boiling water
Zipper-top plastic bags to hold ingredients for mixing and melting
Scissors for cutting a hole in the plastic bag for pouring
Containers for the finished balms

BEES & HONEY

Bees
may travel as far
as 55,000 miles and visit
more than two million
flowers to gather enough
nectar to make just one
pound of honey.

CONTAINERS

FOR BALMS & SOLID LOTIONS

Tube containers: Plastic tube containers can be found in small sizes for lip gloss or in larger sizes for lotions. (The tops of some larger-size tubes are attached to cords so they can be worn as a necklace.)

You can recycle glue stick containers and use them for lotions – just be sure to wash them well. I like to let the remaining glue dry out; then I can pry it out and wash the tubes in warm, sudsy water. Be sure to wash the small plastic piece inside and replace it before pouring in the liquid lotion.

Small jars: Small (1/2 oz.) plastic jars and clear-topped tins are also great for lip gloss. Find them in the fragrance crafting areas of crafts stores or online at packaging suppliers. For larger amounts, 1 oz. and 2 oz. plastic jars give you more space for decorating. Small glass jars that held samples of jam and baby food jars can be recycled for balms.

PACKAGING

BALM CONTAINERS

Stickers with motifs are a quick favorite for decorating containers. Alphabet stickers for adding the child's name and border stickers that wrap around the small jars are also fun to use.

Decorative paper and self-adhesive **glitter papers** can be pre-cut by an adult. Children can decorate with them and glue them on the jar tops and around the tubes. Glue **small plastic charms** on the jar tops as accents.

MAKING THE BALM BASE

I suggest an adult make the balm base, then cut it into pieces and allow children to add the other ingredients. *Tip:* The balm base melts faster and is easier to work with if you use the plastic bag melting method, especially if you're working with a large group of children.

Here's How

1. Melt the beeswax in the almond oil. Use a foil dish or a clean tin can with the top crimped to form a pouring spout. Place the container in a saucepan with water. (An electric frying pan with water works well when you're in a classroom.) Use caution! **Never** melt the mixture over direct heat.
2. When the beeswax is melted, pour the mixture into a plastic container and let solidify.
3. When cool and solid, cut into small pieces for the children to use for balm making.

MAKING BALMS
Zipper-top Plastic Bag Method

1. Place the amount of balm base (see above) that the recipe calls for in a zipper-top plastic bag. Add the additives and close the bag tightly. *Option:* Place almond oil, beeswax, and additives in the bag and close tightly. (A child can do this.)

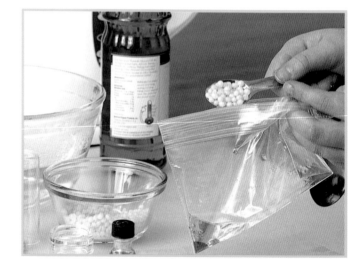

2. Place the bag in a bowl of very hot water (about as hot as a cup of freshly made tea), and leave to melt the ingredients. Take the bag out of the water and gently mix by kneading the bag. If working with a large group of children, prepare a cup of hot water for each child. (You can use an electric kettle to provide the hot water.) **One adult** should supervise **no more than three or four children** at a time for this activity.

3. As soon as the ingredients are melted and mixed well, cut off one of the bottom corners of the bag and pour the mix into the container. If the ingredients have started to harden, you can still squeeze the mixture out into the container. **Do not** move the container until the mixture has solidified completely. *Tip:* Cleaning up spills is easy once the balm has solidified.

Alternate Method

4. Place all the ingredients in a foil pan. Place the pan in an electric frying pan filled with water. Heat the water and let the ingredients melt. Use a craft stick for stirring.

As soon as the lip balm is solidified, it's ready to use.

AN INTERESTING USE OF FRAGRANCE

Aromatherapy is used in Japanese office buildings. Rosemary and lemon scents are believed to help increase productivity, while jasmine and chamomile help employees relax in lounges and dining rooms.

Solid Perfume

This solid perfume recipe contains a lot of fragrance oil – it makes the balm softer and very fragrant. To use perfumed balm, rub your fingers in the perfume, then on your wrist. The warmth of your skin helps release the fragrances. Colorants are not added to solid perfume.

BASIC SOLID PERFUME RECIPE

2 parts grated beeswax

3 parts almond oil

1 part fragrance oil

INVENT A SCENT

The magic of fragrance blending is a centuries-old skill, and making solid perfume is a great activity to do with children after they've invented their own scent blends. Blending scents to create lasting perfumes is not difficult. Children have fun naming their unique blends.

70

FRAGRANCE & MOOD

A fragrant bath may be the perfect way to improve your mood! Using a fragrance to change your mood is called Aromatherapy, and its use dates back to ancient times. It is believed that the scents of plants that are contained in their essential oils affect our emotional and physical well-being.

Many essential oils have specific effects and qualities attributed to them. Here are some examples:
Peaceful, relaxing scents - Lavender, chamomile, tangerine, rose
Energizing scents - Peppermint, lemon, lime, jasmine, honey
Stimulating, uplifting scents - Orange, mint

HELPFUL HINTS
for Fragrance Blending

- Clear and refresh your sense of smell by sniffing a bag of freshly ground coffee when creating the blend.

- Children will naturally choose scents they find most appealing. Some enjoy warm, yummy scents, while others love refreshing, clean scents.

- Some scents are natural blenders and mix well with scents from other scent categories. Examples include: lime, peppermint, lavender, rose, jasmine, vanilla, cinnamon, and honey.

EXAMPLES OF FRAGRANCE BLENDS

Here are some perfume blends that were named by their 10- and 11-year-old creators (boys and girls):

Hug from Grandma - 2 parts lavender, 1 part vanilla

Sunny Lemon - 2 parts lemon, 1 part vanilla

Delicious - 2 parts vanilla, 1 part chocolate, 1 part watermelon

Fruity Air - 4 parts mango, 2 parts pink grapefruit, 1 part lime

Running in a Field - 2 parts cucumber, 2 parts raspberry

HOW TO MAKE YOUR OWN FRAGRANCES

1. Gather some fragrance oils. Place a few drops of different fragrance oils on a small piece of paper towel. Count the number of drops of each fragrance oil you use and record them.

2. Place the paper towel in a plastic bag to let the fragrance oils blend for a few hours. Evaluate the fragrance blend by sniffing and recording the results.

Lip Balms

This is another favorite project for children – if you use sports motifs for decorating and leave the coloring out, boys also enjoy making lip balm. The recipes use the balm base (see the recipe below). An adult can make it ahead of time and let children add flavoring and coloring. Each recipe makes one or two 1/2 oz. containers of lip balm. The amount of lipstick needed to color the lip balm is very little; use a toothpick to remove a small amount.

LIP BALM BASE RECIPE

1 part beeswax

2 parts almond oil

Melt together, using the plastic bag method or the alternate method (foil container in an electric frying pan).

Cocoa-Mint Lip Gloss

Chocolate adds flavor and the cocoa butter in the chocolate adds extra softening qualities. The chocolate will also color the lip gloss; the addition of lipstick makes a nice red-brown hue.

1 heaping teaspoon lip balm base

6 drops peppermint flavoring

1/2 teaspoon grated milk chocolate

Optional: Lipstick to color

Honey-Peppermint Lip Smackers

Honey and peppermint make a lip-smacking balm.

1 heaping teaspoon lip balm base

6 drops peppermint flavoring

1/2 teaspoon liquid honey

Optional: Lipstick to color

Wet Your Whistle Lip Balm

The candy powder (the type that comes in the paper straws) adds flavor and a strong color to the balm.

1 heaping teaspoon lip balm base

6 drops spearmint flavoring

Optional: 1/2 teaspoon red candy powder

AN INTERESTING USE OF FRAGRANCE

Seiko,
the Japanese clock
and watch manufacturer,
makes an alarm clock that
releases the invigorating scents
of eucalyptus and pine before
the alarm rings.

Solid Lotions

Boys love this Bug-Be-Gone lotion, and Glitter Sticks are a big hit with girls. The most expensive item to buy is the container, so recycling glue stick containers works well for larger group projects. (Once you ask family and friends to save them for you, you will get lots!) The recipes are written with the idea of making the lotion base ahead of time. (An adult can do this.) Children can mix fragrance oils and additives to the lotion base to make approximately 1 oz. of lotion, which is enough to fill a small jar or a large tube container. Use the Zipper-Top Plastic Bag Method or the Alternate Method shown at the beginning of this section.

SOLID LOTION BASE RECIPE

1 part beeswax

2 parts almond oil

Vitamin E - one capsule for every ounce of almond oil

Bug-Be-Gone Lotion

Lotion Base - 2 tablespoons

10 drops citronella fragrance oil

10 drops lavender fragrance oil

Glitter Stick

Lotion Base - 2 tablespoons

10 drops orange fragrance oil

10 drops lavender fragrance oil

1/4 teaspoon cosmetic grade glitter powder

Fragrant Powders

Many easy-to-find ingredients make effective, absorbent, safe bath powders for personal use. If you're working with a large group of children, let them mix personal amounts of powder in zipper-top plastic bags.

Instructions follow on page 76.

WHAT YOU NEED

Powder Bases

Cornstarch, arrowroot powder, and **rice flour** are excellent bases for dusting powders – use them alone or as a blend. You can buy them at grocery and health food stores. Cornstarch is a very fine, white starchy powder made from corn. It soothes skin and is used instead of talcum powder. Cornstarch absorbs oil and grease when used in powder blends. Arrowroot powder and rice flour also can be used in powder blends. Since rice flour can be a bit scratchy on children's delicate skin, it should be used sparingly. **Baby powder** also can be used as a base in powder blends; it can replace arrowroot powder and is more economical.

Baking soda (sodium bicarbonate) is added to powder blends for its softening and deodorizing qualities. it holds the fragrance well.

Other Supplies & Equipment

Fragrance oils for scenting
Glass bowls *or* zipper-top plastic bags, for mixing
Spoons for mixing if you are using a bowl
Measuring cups for measuring powders
Decorative containers for packaging (Use plastic jars, recycled spice jars, or powdered sugar tins.)
Optional: Liquid colorants, for tinting

HOW TO MAKE THEM

1. Measure the powder bases and place in a glass bowl. Mix well.
2. Add the fragrance oil(s) and the liquid colorant(s). Mix well, first with a spoon and then with your hands to completely incorporate the fragrance and break up any lumps that form.

TIP FOR USING COLORANTS

It takes a lot of mixing to incorporate a colorant into the powder base. To make it easier for children (who may not have the persistence the job requires), I use this method: Take 1/4 cup of powder base and add 10 to 20 drops colorant. Mix well to make a concentrated colored powder. Have children add 1 teaspoon of this concentrated color mix to their powder for a lovely, light pale hue.

Fairy Dust Powder

This sweet blend adds a sparkle to the skin. It's a big favorite with little girls.

WHAT YOU NEED

Makes 1 cup

1/2 cup cornstarch
1/2 cup baby powder
1/2 teaspoon cosmetic grade soap glitter
10 drops lavender fragrance oil
8 drops orange fragrance oil
6 drops rose fragrance oil
Optional: 4 drops red color *or* 1 teaspoon concentrated colored powder

PACKAGING

1. Place in a plastic jar. Place a powder puff pad in the jar to apply the body powder.
2. Decorate the jar with self-adhesive glitter paper, border stickers, and hearts cut from the glitter paper. ❏

Honey Dust

A delightful-smelling powder that's packaged in a plastic shaker jar children can make themselves.

WHAT YOU NEED

Makes 1 cup

1/2 cup arrowroot powder *or* baby powder

1/2 cup cornstarch

15 drops honey fragrance oil

15 drops rose fragrance oil

Optional: 6 drops orange colorant *or* 1 teaspoon concentrated colored powder

PACKAGING

1. Drill the lid of the plastic jar with holes to create the shaker top. (Children love using a hand drill to make the holes. **Do not** use a hammer and nail – that can shatter a plastic lid.)
2. Place a gold seal sticker over the holes to prevent the powder from coming out in transport or giving as a gift. Include instructions to simply peel off the seal to be able to shake out the powder.
3. Cut a piece of rainbow paper for the label. Add border stickers and bee stickers to accent. ❏

Stinky Sneaker Powder

Sprinkle this powder in sneakers in the evening to keep them fresh and shake out the excess in the morning. The baking soda deodorizes; the cornstarch absorbs excess moisture.

WHAT YOU NEED

3/4 cup baking soda

1/4 cup cornstarch

Fragrance oils: 10 drops lavender, 10 drops lemon

PACKAGING

1. Place powder in a plastic powder shaker.
2. Decorate a piece of tan paper with a rubber stamp and stickers and attach to jar. ❏

Packaging Your Products

Children can have lots of fun making the packages for their handmade fragrance crafts and soaps. The photographs in this book show a variety of packaging ideas using stickers, colored papers, and other easily found materials.

PACKAGING HINTS

Wrapping Soaps

- Wrap soaps with plastic wrap before packaging – it keeps them fresh and keeps the fragrance from dispersing. Plastic wrap also prevents soap from marring or dampening the decorative packaging.
- If glycerin soap is not wrapped, it will dry out and white crystals will form. (The white crystals, though unsightly, are harmless and do not affect the performance of the soap.)
- After the soap is removed from the mold, let it come to room temperature. Use a cling-type plastic wrap and tightly wrap your soap, taping the ends neatly at the back with clear cellophane tape.

Choosing Containers

- For safety's sake, use plastic containers for bath products that will be used in and around the bath and shower. Many crafts stores and bathroom shops stock plastic containers; kitchen stores are also a good place to look.

Labeling Your Products

- Label all fragrance-crafted products for identification. For example, the Bath Biscuits look and smell so yummy someone may be tempted to take a bite. (It won't hurt them – they will just think you are the worst cook ever!)
- Include instructions for use as needed.
- Laminated labels stay fresh-looking even in the high humidity of a steamy bathroom. A hand-crank laminating and adhesive application system is excellent for quickly and easily applying and protecting your labels. Clear packing tape can also be used to cover labels before gluing them on containers.

Storage

- Store fragrance crafted products out of direct light in a cool, dry place.

FAVORITE PACKAGING MATERIALS

Cellophane, both clear cellophane bags and clear cellophane that comes on a roll give a professional look to your projects. The bags are a bit more expensive. Use clear tape for an invisible seam when working with cellophane.

Decorative papers are easy to find in a large variety of colors and designs. You can make your own decorative bubble paper by following the simple steps on the next page.

Paper door hangers create wonderful little windowed packages inexpensively. Find them at crafts stores.

Stickers are available in a huge array of motifs and colors, and they are easy and economical when working with a large group. I especially like border stickers and alphabet stickers.

Ribbon accents that are inexpensive include paper curling ribbon, torn or cut fabric strips, tulle, and raffia.

Felt-tip pens and gel pens in bright colors are used for the lettering on labels – just choose a color that complements the theme. Teach the "dot lettering" technique to add an extra decorative element that is easy.

Decorative edge scissors and punches give professional-looking results and are easy to use.

Shaped novelty erasers are great! They are super cheap, soft, and safe to use in soaps and as colorful decorations. Look for them in toy departments, dollar stores, and party supply outlets.

Plastic charms make great inexpensive, colorful accents.

Small colored paper bags, sold at party supply outlets, are an easy wrap.

Adhesives are needed for applying labels and attaching trims and accents – a low temperature glue gun, clear tape, glue sticks, and glue dots are all good choices.
- A hand-cranked laminating and adhesive application system is excellent for quickly applying labels.
- Plain self-adhesive white labels (the kind you can find in stationery and office supply stores) are inexpensive and can be decorated with stickers

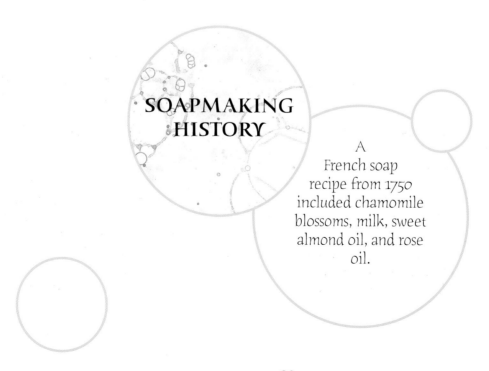

SOAPMAKING HISTORY

A French soap recipe from 1750 included chamomile blossoms, milk, sweet almond oil, and rose oil.

MAKING BUBBLE PAPER

This is a simple, fun, and unusual form of decorative paper that can be produced by the children for decorating their fragrance crafts.

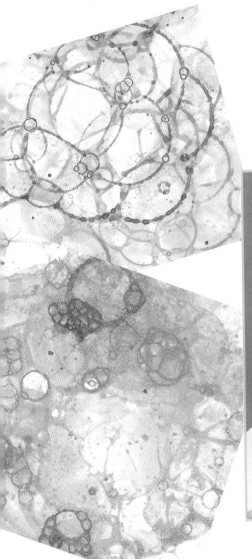

WHAT YOU NEED

- **Prepared Paint** - Thin drawing inks or acrylic paints with water (use equal amounts paint and water). Add a squirt of liquid soap and stir.
- **Paper** - Paper with a smooth, shiny surface works best, but a plain white paper also can be used.
- **Plastic bowls**, one for each paint color. Use disposable or recycled plastic containers.
- **Plastic straws**, one for each paint color. Cut the straws in half and give each child a set. Be sure they throw them away after they make their paper.
- **Blank newsprint or wax paper** to cover the workspace so splashes and popping bubbles won't stain your table.
- **Aprons** to protect clothing. (The bubbles tend to splatter.)

HOW TO MAKE IT

1. Line up the plastic containers – one for each color – and fill one-third full with prepared paint. Place a straw for each color beside each bowl.
2. Beginning with the one color, use the straw to gently blow into the prepared paint, filling the container with colored bubbles. Keep blowing until the bubbles have risen about 1" over the top of the container.
3. Place the paper on the bubbles gently to make a print.
4. Repeating the process with the other colors until the sheet is covered with the bubble design.
   - You need to blow the bubbles in the prepared color each time you make a print.
   - Let the bubbles that stick to the paper pop to create the clearest bubble images.

Collections for Gift Giving

This section contains suggestions for combining the projects in this book to create collections for giving. You can package your collections in a basket, a box, a bowl, or a bag with a see-through window. Nice additions for gift collections include brightly colored washcloths, tub toys, and soap dishes. When giving your handmade bath products, be sure to label them clearly and include instructions for use.

WHAT IS A LOOFAH?

A loofah is a light tan-colored tubular sponge you can use in the bath. It comes from a plant that looks something like a cucumber when growing; another name for it is "washrag gourd." When the gourd is ripe, the skin is peeled off to reveal a fibrous sponge that can be cleaned and dried in the sun. A loofah will last a long time if allowed to dry after each use.

Different spellings include "lofah," "luffa," and "lufa."

The Princess Collection

Bubbling Jelly (see page 47)

Glitter Bubbling Bath Oil (see page 48)

Loofah Heart Soap (see page 37)

Fairy Dust Powder (see page 76)

Glitter Stick (see page 74)

Lip Gloss (see pages 72-73)

Heart-shaped Cookie Cutter Soap
(see pages 28-29)

Blue Collection

Wake-up Sun & Dream-on Moon Bath Fizzies
(see page 54)

Cookie Cutter Duck Soap (see pages 28-29)

Glitter Fish Soaps (see pages 16-17)

Blue Scrubby Soap (see page 36)

Rainbow Collection

Fruity Rainbow Bath Salts (see page 62)

Crayon Soaps (see page 19)

Rainbow Soap (see page 35)

Oopsie-daisy Soaps (see page 34)

Two-toned Soap (see page 24)

Creepy Crawlies Collection

Fossil Soap
(see page 40)

Swamp Bubbles
(not shown – see page 46)

Bug-Be-Gone Lotion
(see page 74)

Treasure Soap
(see page 32)

Dragonfly Soap-on-a-Rope
(see page 38)

Dinosaur Egg Surprise Fizzy
(see page 56)

SOAP-MAKING HISTORY

Historians believe soap was made in prehistoric times. They think people discovered this slippery substance that created bubbles while cooking over open pits when they observed what happened when fat and ashes combined.

**DINOSAUR EGG
BATH FIZZY**

Place a dinosaur egg in your
bath to hatch a fragrant,
bubbling pool of fun!
Who will you find in your egg?

Bug·be·gone
Lotion

Yummy Scents Collection

Bubble Gum Soap (see page 43)

Lollipop Soap (see page 30)

Bath Bon-Bons (see page 55)

Candy Cane Bath Salts (see page 65)

Cute Critters Collection

Foaming Honey Bath Oil (see page 48)

Honey Lip Gloss (see page 73)

Honey Dust (see page 77)

Solid Perfume in a Butterfly Jar (see page 70)

Bug-Be-Gone Lotion (see page 74)

Natural Handmade Collection

Bath Biscuits (see page 58)

Cherry Pie Soap (see pages 22-23)

Chocolate Milk Bath (see page 64)

Stinky Sneaker Powder (see page 77)

For Parents & Teachers

The same advice for working with large groups of children applies whether you are hosting a fragrance crafting party, teaching in a classroom, or sharing at a church or activity group. After years of teaching both adults and children, I have found I like to use a "stations" format with large groups.

The benefits of a stations format are many:

- Stations allow children to move around to make and package a selection of fragrance-crafted projects.
- The stations format keeps all the children busy with no time to get bored or frustrated – they're not all standing around the microwave waiting their turn.
- There's less equipment to set up.
- Children produce more projects at their own pace in the allotted time. They will have a high success rate and take home finished projects.

This method of working with children does, however, require adult supervisors for each station. I have never had a problem with getting adult volunteers, especially if they're invited to make the projects! Remember that the challenge of teaching involves more than simply showing a technique – you also should generate interest and enthusiasm, and be patient.

SETTING UP THE SPACE

This is a get-up-and-move-around type of class. Make sure there is enough room for the children to get around comfortably. Have one adult volunteer for each station. Stations can accommodate three to six participants, depending on the project.

Be familiar with the recipes, products, and instructions. *Always* try them ahead of time to anticipate any problems.

1. Protect tables with newsprint or wax paper for easy cleanup.
2. Prepare each station and make sure all equipment and supplies are accessible. Have laminated recipes and instructions at each station for the children to copy. Provide choices in fragrances, colors, and packaging accents so they can personalize their projects. Have finished samples available.
3. Talk about all safety considerations.
4. Demonstrate each product at each station to show the steps. Show the children and adult supervisors that all the step-by-step instructions are posted at each station. Ask if there are questions after each demonstration.
5. Provide children with a "home station" where, as projects are completed, they can pile up their finished projects. Be sure proper containers are available for children to take their projects home. (One example – uncovered bath fizzies on a rainy day can result in some very unhappy children.)

HOW TO SET UP A FRAGRANCE CRAFTING PARTY OR CLASS

Here's a sample setup using the stations format for a fragrance crafting class or party with a winter holiday theme. This party or class can accommodate 20 children, both boys and girls, and requires five adult supervisors.

The room is set up with five stations, detailed below. Four children can work at each station with one adult supervisor and rotate around the room to finish all the projects. Make sure all the necessary equipment and supplies are at each station.

Pictured above: Unmolding a bath fizzy.

Pictured below: Unmolding soap.

STATION 1

Soapmaking Project - Snowflake Foam-shaped Soaps

Equipment - Laminated recipe and general step-by-step instructions, microwave oven or hot plate, heat-resistant glass measuring cups, wax paper

Supplies - Snowflake foam shapes, clear glycerin soap base, peppermint fragrance, soap glitter

At the packaging station, the soaps can be placed on a piece of decorated card and in a cellophane bag. Close the bag with a white ribbon bow or a piece of snowflake garland.

STATION 2

Bath Salts Project -
Candy Cane Layered Bath Salts

Equipment - Laminated recipe and general step-by-step instructions, spoons, glass jars with lids, tube containers
Supplies - Salts, fragrances, colorants
At the packaging station, add a charm, label, and ribbon to accent.

STATION 3

Bath Fizzies Project - Snowball Fizzies

Equipment - Laminated recipe and general step-by-step instructions, mixing bowls, mister bottle with water, measuring cups, wax paper, pieces of cardboard
Supplies - Fizzies ingredients, fragrances, soap glitter
At the packaging station, place paper shreds and fizzies in a cellophane bag and label. The children will need to wait until the bath fizzies are hard (at the end of the class) to place them in the packages.

Pictured below: Mixing bath salts.

STATION 4

Lip Balm Project -
Wet Your Whistle Lip Balm

Equipment - Laminated recipe and general step-by-step instructions, electric kettle, five tea cups, gallon water container filled with water, zipper-top plastic bags, scissors, containers
Supplies - Lip balm base (make this ahead of time), flavoring, additives
At the packaging station, add stickers to accent.

STATION 5

Packaging and Finishing

Supplies - Self-adhesive blank labels, colored pens, glue gun and glue sticks, laminating and adhesive machine, plastic charms, paper ribbon, coordinating decorative paper (pre-cut to size) plus anything else you wish to include.

Metric Conversion Chart

Inches to Millimeters and Centimeters

Inches	MM	CM	Inches	MM	CM
1/8	3	.3	2	51	5.1
1/4	6	.6	3	76	7.6
3/8	10	1.0	4	102	10.2
1/2	13	1.3	5	127	12.7
5/8	16	1.6	6	152	15.2
3/4	19	1.9	7	178	17.8
7/8	22	2.2	8	203	20.3
1	25	2.5	9	229	22.9
1-1/4	32	3.2	10	254	25.4
1-1/2	38	3.8	11	279	27.9
1-3/4	44	4.4	12	305	30.5

Yards to Meters

Yards	Meters	Yards	Meters
1/8	.11	3	2.74
1/4	.23	4	3.66
3/8	.34	5	4.57
1/2	.46	6	5.49
5/8	.57	7	6.40
3/4	.69	8	7.32
7/8	.80	9	8.23
1	.91	10	9.14
2	1.83		

Index

Index